S0-ABA-653

pluckyfluff
Handspun Revolution

Pluckyfluff Publishing
1133 Locust Avenue
Placerville, California 95667
email: pluckyfluff@hotmail.com
www.pluckyfluff.com

Copyright 2005 by Lexi Boeger

All right reserved. No part of this book may be produced or transmitted in any form or by any means, electronic or mechanical, including photocopying, recording, or by any information storage and retrieval system, without the written permission of Pluckyfluff Publishing, except where permitted by law.

Printed in Canada

ISBN 0-9767252-0-7
LCCN 2005902407

First Edition

rev·o·lu·tion

1) motion of any figure about a center or axis

2) a fundamental change in the way of thinking
about or visualizing something

On My Terms....

The yarns and techniques illustrated in this book are described with a terminology that is partially fabricated by me. Most of these techniques were new and had no established vocabulary to describe them, so I simply used words that I felt reflected the nature of the subject. The tiny bits of balled up wool that stick to the yarn just beg to be called *nublets*! Or *nubbies* if you prefer. Those little coiled sections look just like beehives to me, and so I named them that. I have seen a few of these terms defined differently in other resources and I apologize ahead of time if this causes any offense or confusion. However, I find it hard to apply dry or tedious language to such a vibrant activity. Spinning is intrinsically energetic and needs energetic language to describe it.

But don't take my word for it...
In this same spirit, don't use my terms if they don't sound right to you. If your nubbie is really a boppie, or your beehive a bunbun, then so be it. You spin it, you name it.

A Little Bit About This Book

The instructions in this book assume a basic knowledge of spinning on the part of the reader. If you don't know how to spin, check your local yarn shops for classes. It is very important to master the basics of spinning first. Challenge yourself to spin perfectly straight, even and balanced yarns. This is the only route to truly creative spinning. **You have to understand the rules before you can break them.**

This book is purposefully simple. It is written in a spartan manner because I believe that these yarns should act as inspiration to launch you into your own discoveries rather than a strict recipe for a specific yarn. You will get the gist of how I made them, however you should find your own best way of achieving the look you want. What worked well for me may not work well for you. Or you may start to do something the way I suggested and stumble upon a much easier way. So be open to these things when you are spinning your yarns. Don't get upset if it's not turning out the way you expected it to, it NEVER does. **It is when the yarn diverges from your intentions that discovery and innovation happen.** Most of the techniques listed in this book are the result of a mistake. So when something unexpected happens while you are spinning, or you begin to lose a little control of it, don't stop and fix it. Let it become a part of the yarn and more; learn from it. But don't stop there, push it a step further and very soon you will be creating yarns that you could never have imagined.

The yarns in this book should serve as a stepping stone to your own unique yarn making. By the end of this book you will be discovering your own techniques and yarns that will far surpass these. Do not trap yourself by trying to follow every instruction so closely that you block out your own creativity. Go where your yarn takes you, embrace the unexpected and recognize that mistakes are not mistakes, they are possibilities.

UNCOMMON THREAD

A few years ago a friend of mine taught me how to crochet. I liked it well enough, but found my hands always wanting to go faster than the hook. More importantly, I felt so much more exuberance ogling the different yarns rather than actually crocheting them. I always felt like the finished project was never quite as nice as the yarn was in its' original state. Then I accidentally bought a handspun yarn and it was all over. I say accidentally because it was an unprepossessing 2 ply yarn that blended in with all the other yarns. But when I got it home it just felt different in my hands. It was subtle, but it had so much more...I don't know how to put it.. *integrity* than mass-made yarn. I went back to the store and said "what was that???". Handspun. I had never even heard of it before.

Luckily for me the owner of the little yarn shop in my town offered spinning classes and I signed up. I knew I was going to love spinning before I even attended one class, but after that first day the deal was sealed. This was no weekend spinner class either. We started out with a dirty, stinky fleece. We washed, washed, washed, then carded, carded, carded. Then we learned the dropspindle, then plying on the dropspindle and then finally, after weeks of this, we got to actually SPIN. On an actual wheel.

Raw fleece, washing, carding. I think it's very important to learn these things first because you gain an appreciation not just for what a yarn *is*, but what it *was*. You also have that feeling that you are not vastly separated from people in the past. A hundred, a thousand years ago, you stood over the hot water, washing the wool.

So what is it about handspun yarn that makes it so compelling? It's beautiful, surely. It feels nice. Looks nice. But what is the real attraction that people feel towards handspun yarn? I think it's that each yarn tells a story.

Knitting with handspun yarn is like reading a book. Each inch that comes along the needle has a different character, totally unique and different from all the other inches in its length. As you work through the yarn you never know what to expect next. Sometimes it goes along smoothly for a long time, then POP! You are startled by a big blob with sparks of sparkle, or a menacing inky shadow with trailing fibers lurks across your needle. A handspun yarn also tells you a story about the person who made it. You run your fingers down the yarn, and you feel the impressions made by the hand of the spinner. It's like a long distance handshake.

Handspun yarn also engenders the spirit of collaboration. A project made from handspun yarn is actually made by two people: the spinner and the knitter/crocheter. At times the knitter dictates the design and at other times the yarn dictates the next move. There is an exciting play between the whims of the spinner and the intention of the knitter, and vice versa. In the end, you have a final creation that from start to finish is cared for, created, honest and whole

WHEELS

The number one spinning question that I get asked is: "what wheel do you use?". This is a natural enough question to ask when you look at these yarns. I wish I could say that there was a perfect wheel out there for these techniques, but unfortunately that is not the case. Current spinning wheels are designed for traditional yarns, and as such it can be quite difficult to produce unorthodox yarns on them. Until the wheel makers catch up with the new trends in spinning, a great deal of patience will be necessary to make these yarns. They will get hooked up, caught on guides, be hard to get through the hole and probably be too big for the bobbin. Many of these yarns are made in spite of the wheel, rather than with the help of it. So before you sit down to spin, be sure you've had your morning coffee or, as I find helpful in the evening, a nice glass of wine. Take a deep breath, toss all expectations aside and adopt the patience of a samurai, the calmness of Yoda.

Don't let these little speed bumps discourage you though. Any wheel you get is going to be great fun and you will learn to adapt to the tools that you have to work with. Just keep an open mind, be inventive and don't let a little thing like equipment problems stop you from pursuing an idea. There is always a way to make it work, it's simply a matter of experimenting and sticking with it.

There are some things to consider when buying a wheel that can make it a little easier however. These are the top priorities when looking for a wheel to make these yarns:

1) **Large orifice**. For bulky yarns with add-ins, poofs, shag, etc. The bigger the hole the easier they will fit through. 3/4 inch is the largest I've used, but if you find one bigger then go for it. (Note: This size will most likely be on a Bulky Spinner. Bulky Spinners spin much slower than standard wheels and are not very good for making delicate yarns, so there is obviously a trade off here.)

2) **Big guides**. The yarn is constantly catching on the guides and this will be your biggest frustration. Look for

a wheel with large guides. If you can't find one, it is possible to replace the small guides with larger ones from the hardware store, but be careful not to split the wood or drill all the way through the flyer.

Tip: The flyer usually has guides on both sides. You only need one. Remove one set of guides as they are simply an added potential for hang-ups. **Tip 2**: You may want to dip the ends of the guides in wax or epoxy, as the sharp edges tend to catch on some fibers, causing problems.

3) **Quill**. Some wheels come with the option of a "quill" attachment. This is ideal for spinning yarns that have elements that absolutely will not fit through an orifice. I find the quill a little less smooth to spin with than a standard flyer/bobbin set up, but that is just me. I know some people who use it for everything, so this might be a good option for some of you.

4) **Threading hook**. Make sure your wheel comes with one. This will be your best friend. It is a must have for fishing bulky things through the orifice.

Your main decision will be choosing between a standard wheel or a bulky spinner. It is important to assess what your personal tendencies are. A standard wheel has greater speed, efficiency and control, but you will have more hang-ups on the guides and be hand feeding through the orifice more often. A bulky spinner will handle bigger objects in the yarn easily, it makes big, soft flowing yarns and holds much more yarn on the bobbin. However Bulky Spinners tend to spin very slow and are not good for tight or delicate work. Some companies offer a bulky flyer that can be added onto a standard wheel. The ideal combination for the most versatility would be a standard wheel with a quill attachment as well as a bulky flyer attachment.

Tip: Before you invest in a wheel, you may consider trying a dropspindle. It is good for very simple spinning and only costs around $8.00. It is an affordable way to see if you like the process of making your own yarn.

MATERIALS

The sky's the limit as far as materials go when handspinning, but lets cover the basics. What you can't find in your spinning store you can always get on EBAY. Or do an Internet search on "spinning fiber" or "roving" and browse away.

WOOL $

Wool is the most traditional spinning fiber and probably the most loved. There are so many different breeds of wool, all different and wonderful. You should absolutely experiment with as many different types as you can get your hands on.

COTTON $

Short cotton fibers can be tough to spin are but great for spring and summer yarns. Mix it in with other fibers to create texture.

TENCEL $

Fabulous biodegradable fiber of very short strands that is derived from wood pulp. Dye loose tencel and card into your mix for a confetti look.

SILK $$

Comes in hanks, combed or noil. Takes dye very well and is easy to spin.

DOWNY FIBERS $$$-$$$$

Buffalo, Yak, Camel, Musk Ox.... This stuff is as good as cashmere or angora for softness, but short fibers make spinning a challenge so be patient!

ANGORA $$$$

Beginners: be sure to buy already combed, it is very hard to card nicely. Mix this in with wool for a super soft blend and stretch your dollar while you're at it.

CASHMERE $$$$

Tough to spin unless you buy already processed or blended, but ohhh so nice!

ALPACA $$$

Very nice, soft long fiber that is easy to spin. Alpaca comes in a range of beautiful natural colors.

SPARKLE $

There are several different types, try them all and mix them up. They all usually hand dye very well and great pre-dyed colors are available.

PLYING MATERIALS

Here is where you can spend a lot or a little. Do not go spend five bucks on a new spool of sewing thread to ply with! Go to your local thrift stores and I guarantee there will be tons of sewing thread of every vintage and color. But better yet, go to the craft section and look for the big cones of embroidery thread. They usually only cost a buck or two but will last you all year!

MISCELLANEOUS

Be ever watchful for the perfect little thing. Bag of sequins at a garage sale, silk flowers, vintage buttons, twist ties, you name it.

CARDING

Weather you are a long time spinner or just learning, having your own hand carders or drum carder is an absolute must. If you are only spinning with the professionally processed, super combed fibers from the store then you are not only missing a big part of the picture but you are doing yourself a disservice as well. Wool that has been hand carded has a whole different feel. It will be loftier, bouncier and most important: imperfect. If you only take one thing away from this book let it be this: **It is the imperfection of handspun yarn that makes it beautiful.** Hand carding will leave little lumps in the wool that come out in the yarn later giving it character. The fibers feel more resilient and lively since they have not been stressed and subdued by a heavy machine. Carding your own fiber also gives you the opportunity to make something very unique. There are many ways to mix it up.

MIX don't MATCH! Try some of these options when carding:

-Card several different contrasting colors together.
-Mix your fibers- Try wool and tencel, mohair and silk, all of the above and more!
-ADD SOME SPARKLE! You can never have too much sparkle.
-Add something strange. Lint from the dryer, shreds from your Levi's.

Do not be afraid to try something unusual. You have nothing to lose. I was taught that you cannot make an ugly yarn, and I have not seen one yet.

Tip: And I'm giving away one of my big secrets here….
After you have finished carding, carefully remove the little bits of wool, sparkle and fiber that get left behind in the teeth and stash these beautiful gems in a safe place. Do this every time you card and pretty soon you will have the loveliest pile of fiber treasure. Use these to make multi-colored sparkle nubs in your yarn, or save up enough and make a whole beautiful yarn filled with a thousand colors and textures. This is a good habit to have

in general. If you are shuffling through your fiber bags and find a particularly attractive bit of fiber, rescue it and put it in the treasure box. Save little pretty bits from everywhere: home, store, sidewalk and add them to your stash. This not only will make a great yarn, but will also train you to start looking at your surroundings in a new way. **Little tiny things deserve great attention.**

SETTING THE TWIST - For singles

It is very important to set the twist on a single, especially with many of the special techniques talked about in this book. Without setting the twist, all your hard work can be lost!

Set Twist:
After you have filled your bobbin with a single ply yarn, wind it onto your niddy-noddy. Tie each end of the yarn securely through the skein in a figure 8 tied with a tight square knot. Use scrap yarn to tie the skein tightly in each of the four sections on the noddy. This will ensure that your yarn does not get tangled.

Fill a bucket, bowl or sink up with a few inches of VERY HOT water. Take your skein off and submerge it in the water. The hot water will shock the natural fibers and help to set the twist. Let soak 5 minutes. Remove the skein, squeeze out the excess water and put it in the washing machine on the spin cycle to make sure all the water is out.

Now for the most important part! Find a place to stretch the skein. Between the legs of two chairs will work as well as anything. Make sure the yarn is stretched as tight as it will go. Let dry in front of heater or over night.

THE YARNS...

NUBS

Nubs are very easy to make and have many variations and uses. A nub is made by spinning a small chunk of roving or fiber onto a forming yarn at a 90 degree angle. (As opposed slubs, which are incidental lumps that naturally occur in the roving while spinning.)

Pre-Spinning Prep:
Select the fibers that you want to make nubs out of. Pull pieces out approximately 2"x 1" (for a peanut sized nub). Draft the edges out a little. You can use absolutely any fiber for nubs: wool, silk, sparkle, scraps etc. Don't be afraid to experiment!

Time to spin!
Begin spinning a single. When you are ready to add a nub, stop the wheel, draft your base yarn roving out until you have a thin section. Pinch the drafted end of the nub fiber to this thin section of roving and resume spinning. Allow the drafted end of the nub fiber to catch in the thin section of the base fiber. As you spin, the Nub section will want to wrap around the base yarn. Allow it to do this, using your fingers to form the nub around the yarn, molding it like clay. Make sure the Nub fiber is being led in at a 90 degree angle to the base yarn. That's it! Simple.

Try it with different materials for different looks and vary the size of pre-made sections for big and small nubs.
-Smooth Nubs: Use combed rovings.
-Lumpy Nubs: Uncarded wool or fiber
-Mixed materials like down carded with mohair.
-Yarn Scraps
-Straight sparkle fibers.
-Or try my favorite: The fuzz scraped out of your carders after carding many different colors of wool and sparkle.

15

CANDY STRIPE

Select at least two solid colored rovings and one or two different threads (metallic thread looks great on Candy Stripes). Separate the roving into very narrow strips of manageable lengths. Take one strip in each color and stick them back together, forming lengthwise striped sections. Begin spinning these sections into a single along with the thread. To ensure that the thread sits on top of the yarn and does not get twisted inside, spin the wool but let the thread drift on a second behind the twist, laying it on top. You can use an extra finger to keep the thread out of the twist . (see picture below)

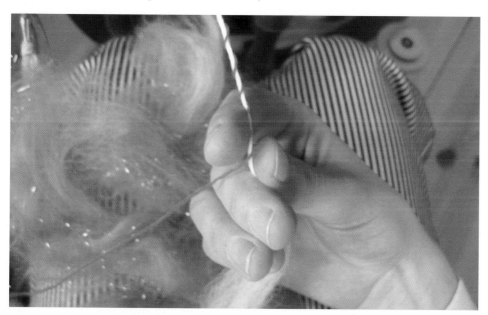

LOOPS

Loops are formed in the plying stage, so a little forethought is needed when spinning the single for this yarn. You can add loops to a solid color yarn for texture, or you can have loops in a contrasting color to the base yarn. If you go with the latter, simply spin a single in one color and sporadically add 4-6 inch sections of a different color. These sections will become the loops when plying. Spin your single, soak and set the twist. Once it is dry, wind it into a ball and prepare to ply.

Choose a good sturdy thread to ply with so it holds the loops securely. Begin plying. When you reach a different colored section stop spinning and form a loop with that section. Pinching the loop at the base, wind the plying thread 2-3 times tightly around the base of the loop where the yarn meets back up with itself. Once the loop is secure, bring the thread back around and lay it along side the base yarn. Continue to ply as before. Repeat at each new colored section.

For extra fun, mix loops with other techniques such as beehives. (see photo at left)

KNOTS
(Far left)

This technique is done on any single ply yarn. While spinning your single, periodically stop, break the roving off and tie a square knot at the end of your spun fiber. Re-attach the roving and continue spinning. Repeat. For a more textural yarn tie several knots in the same place.

Tip: If spinning a thick and thin single, try to tie knots in the thicker sections for the greatest effect.

SCRAPS

Scraps yarn is easiest to spin with hand carded wool since the lofty fibers will readily grab onto the scrap sections. Select a few yarns and threads and wind them into a skein on to your niddy-noddy. Take the skein off and cut through all the threads. Begin cutting every inch or so making a big pile of yarn scraps. Mix these scraps into your carded wool by tossing it like a salad. Pull the wool fibers open with your hands, making sure the scraps are good and tangled with the wool. This will ensure that they stick in the yarn while spinning.

Spin a single from your concoction. Don't try to control it too much- many scraps will fall out but plenty will get caught in the wool.

Tip: This is the perfect use for the leftover yarn from your knitting/crochet projects!

SEQUINS- Three ways

Sequin clusters

Buy solid sequin trims from the sewing store. Single sequin trims are easiest but thick trims make very dramatic clusters. Cut trim into 4 inch sections. Pull 3/4 to an inch worth of sequins off of each end of the cut section leaving the inner strings exposed. You will use these strings to spin the section into your yarn.

Begin spinning a single. Stop the wheel and draft the fiber until a thin spot is created. Make a small split in the fiber at the thin spot and lay the exposed strings from a sequin segment inside the fiber. Commence spinning, trapping the strings and spinning them into the single. When the twist gets to the sequins, pinch the single and, still spinning, allow the sequin strand to wrap around the yarn in a cluster. When you get to the last sequin, stop. Split the roving again, tuck the tail end strings between the fibers and continue spinning sealing the strings inside the yarn. Repeat every few yards.

Spaced Sequins

Spin a single with a pre-strung sequin yarn. You can find these specialty yarns at most yarn shops.

Sporadic Sequins

Hand string sequins onto 12 inch lengths of thread and knot a sequin at each end. While spinning a single, occasionally add a section by the method described above: split the roving, insert the thread to trap it, continue spinning.

SPECKLES

You must have hand carders or a drum carder for this yarn.

Materials:
-Uncarded wool (natural colored wool looks best- black, brown or gray)
-Loose tencel fiber
-Assortment of dyes

Dye the loose tencel with the colors of your choice. The more the better! Let dry.
Card the dyed tencel into the wool by breaking it into little pieces and distributing it evenly while carding.

Spin carded fiber into a thick and thin single.

Tip: You will notice that lots of colorful tencel and wool get lodged in the carders after carding. Don't throw this stuff away! Pluck it out and save it for spectacular nubs!

SUPERSLUB

Pre-Spinning Prep:
Select several different colored combed top rovings. Separate each color into two different sized sections:
- 2 foot strips approximately 1/2 inch wide for the base yarn.
- 3 inch by 1 inch chunks for superslubs. (approximately)

Time to spin!
Spin the base yarn in two or more colors from the long strips. Periodically pause to draft a thin spot in the roving. Select 2 to 3 of the small chunks in different colors and lay them side by side forming one big piece. Pre-draft the ends of this new segment so that it will spin into the base yarn easily. Lay one end into the thin spot in the base yarn and commence spinning being careful not to let the twist go beyond the slub until it is spun good and tight. Spin a few inches of base yarn behind the slub. Carefully wind the slub onto the bobbin without letting it untwist. Repeat every few feet.

Tip: The superslubs will want to untwist when you take this yarn off the bobbin, so be sure you keep a tight rein on it until it is securely on the niddy noddy. **You absolutely must set the twist and stretch this yarn!** (See page 12 for setting the twist)

SPIDER'S NEST

Materials:
- Fine combed roving in spider web hues. Look for a blend of wool/silk/cashmere for a fine sheen.
- Black, brown or gray wool for the spider bodies. (lofty short fiber is best for fuzzy spiders)
- White shimmer/sparkle fiber for spider egg nests.
- Spider legs: Black craft whiskers, stiff metallic thread, ultra thin wire or any other material that is stiff, yet will hold a bend.

Pre-Spinning Prep: (See instructions for Nubs page 15)
Separate the spider body roving and white shimmer as you would to make Nubs.
Pre-separate your base yarn roving into easily spun skinny strips.
Pre-cut your spider legs into 2 inch long sections.

Time to spin!
Begin spinning a single. Warm up with a spider egg nest by spinning a small section of white shimmer on as a Nub (see page 13). Spin a few yards before adding another nub. Time for a spider! Draft the base yarn fiber out until a fairly thin area is formed. (Thin areas attract more twist than thick ones.) Make a split the fiber in at this point and insert 4 spider legs, centering them in the opening. Bring the fiber back together sandwiching the legs inside. Grab a prepared section of the brown spider wool and pinch the drafted end to the point where the legs protrude from the yarn. Begin spinning and form the spider body just as you would a Nub. It will be necessary to guide the fiber over and under the legs, making a rough figure 8. Watch as you are forming the spider body that the legs stay perpendicular to the base yarn. If they get crooked, bring the body fiber up under the low side to straighten it out, then back over the high side, etc. To secure the spider body to the yarn, spin a little of the spider fiber under the legs and down into the base yarn. Take a moment to pluck the spider body fibers up to hide the criss-cross pattern. Repeat making nests and spiders every few yards.
*You may need to hand wind the spiders through the orifice and onto your spool as they might get hung up on the guides. Once the spool is full, unwind your yarn into a skein and set the twist. While the skein is drying on the stretcher, go through and put a bend in the legs of each spider so they are not sticking straight out.

FUZZING

This is a very simple way to make soft and fuzzy yarns! This technique will not work with finely processed combed rovings or cotton. It works best with downy fibers (Yak, Buffalo) or short to medium fibered wools that have been picked or hand carded and retain a certain sponginess.

There are two ways to make this yarn: with a thread core and without. It is a good idea to use a thread or skinny yarn core until you feel comfortable with the technique. Once you get the hang of it a core is not necessary. Choose a material for your core that has some grab to it like a mohair yarn or a rough metallic thread. If it's too smooth the fiber will not stick to it.

Spin a lead section with your core thread and fiber of choice. With one hand, gently hold the thread between your thumb and index finger. Hold the fiber in your other hand. You will use one hand to tease the fibers while the other hand holds on to the forming yarn and guides the twist. To tease or "fuzz" the fibers, briskly tug the fibers between both hands (one hand always on the core!) while spinning, allowing them to grab onto the core thread. Continue to tug them off the core, then spin them back on again loosely. You are basically fluffing the fibers up between both hands and allowing the loose fibers to gently attach to the core thread. One hand holds the core, the forming yarn and the fiber while the other hand teases the fiber out. Imagine that both hands are fighting over the fiber, the "fuzzing" hand gets it partially away but the spinning hand always gets it back and lays it on the core.

MOHAIRY

See "FUZZING" instructions page 29.

This is Fuzzing for Mohair and is very fun and easy! It is easiest when the Mohair is loose and fluffy, so look for fiber that has been picked or carded but not combed. If all you have is combed fiber take the time to pre-fluff it before spinning. You can do this by hand carding it or simply teasing it with your hands making a lofty pile.

Since Mohair has a transparent quality to it, try adding some sparkle fiber and spinning on a metallic thread core. Fuzz the Mohair way out, don't be shy! Mohair Fibers are very long and can take quite a lot of teasing while still adhering to the core thread.

TORNADO

Choose several threads or yarns for this yarn. The more delicate the better, as they will be more lofty and you will be able to see the core yarn through them. Begin spinning a single (wool is easiest). Add your yarns and threads in, spin a few inches to secure. Continue spinning. Hold all threads and yarns in your drafting hand and pull out 2 feet or so from the spools. While you are spinning the single, pile the threads/yarns onto the twisting fiber, winding them on loosely and quickly.
Once you have spun all the slack, pull two more feet out and spin on as before. Repeat.

This is another one of those yarns that will tend to get hung up on the guides. You will have to do a lot of hand winding so be patient!

BIRDSNEST- Elastic core yarn

Note: Spinning is a "handed" activity, and in many of these right-left preference actions you may be "goofy". Try stretching the elastic with each hand to find out what feels most comfortable.

Elastic, or shirring thread, can easily be found in any sewing store. The color of thread is not important as it is spun inside the yarn and won't show.

This yarn is basically a simple single spun on an elastic core thread. Any fiber will work, however easily drafted wool is the easiest to manage.

Start by attaching the elastic thread to the lead string along with the roving. Begin spinning a single, drafting your roving alongside the thread making sure to cover the thread completely with the fiber. Do not let the elastic wrap around the outside of the single. Once you get going, begin stretching the elastic thread as tightly as you can while drafting the fiber next to it and allowing it to spin around the elastic core. An easy way to do this is to pinch the single and elastic near the orifice with one hand while simultaneously stretching the elastic to it's maximum with the other. Then, keeping a tight hold of the stretched elastic with one hand, slide your other hand down drafting and applying fiber as you go.

Tip: If you wrap the thread around your pinky, as in knitting, it will be easier to control tension.

Repeat this process throughout, maintaining an even tension for the whole yarn. (Or not! You could stretch in some sections, relax in others, to create a yarn that is both flat and curly).

The main principal here is that the yarn is made curly by spinning the roving over tightly stretched elastic. The tighter the elastic thread is stretched during spinning the springier and curlier the yarn will be.

FELTED YARN
(Single ply)

Begin by spinning a single in wool. For an interesting yarn try spinning in some nubs (see Nubs page 13) or include some sections of a unique novelty yarn. If you're feeling really frisky, try spinning in some sequins or beads.

Once your yarn is spun you will need to set the twist before felting. (See page 10 for setting the twist in singles). After the twist is set, lay your skein out in an "O" and tie it securely every 5 inches with a non-felting cotton string.

Time to felt!
Put the tied skein in the washing machine with a little soap and set to HOT with the roughest agitation. After it runs through the cycle take the skein out and untie the ties. You will need to carefully separate the yarn where the ties were, as they may have tried to felt to each other. Once the entire skein is separated and not sticking to itself anywhere, tie new ties on every 5 inches and put in the wash for another cycle. Repeat until it is felted to your desired texture.

To untangle, carefully remove the ties and separate all the strands. Untie the beginning and end of the yarn from the skein and slowly wind into a ball from the outside end. It will seem like it's tangled but it shouldn't be if your ties were on tightly. You will have to gently un-stick the yarn from itself as you unwind it.

Felted yarn is great for making sturdy projects like handbags or dolls.

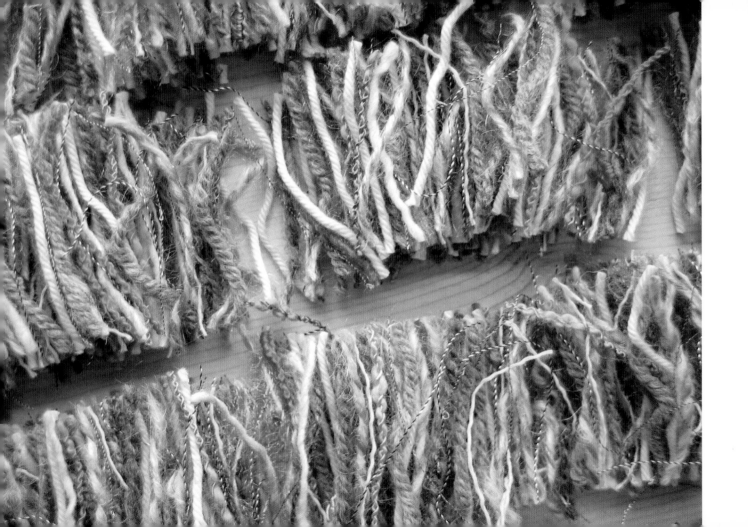

SHAG

You will need to spin on a Quill or a Bulky Spinner with a large orifice.

Pre- spinning prep:
-Choose 5 to 6 styles of yarn and thread for your shag. Look for variable sizes and textures as well as interesting color combinations. Try mixing thick and thin yarns with simple string or a little sparkle thread for flare. This is a great use for all those remnants from your knitting projects! Once you have chosen your yarns, lay them out on the floor and bring the ends of each one together and tie a knot.
Now you will need to make a skein of them. Use your niddy noddy to do this. Hold on to the knotted end and begin wrapping the yarns and threads around the noddy until the bunch is approximately 3 to 4 inches in diameter. Cut the yarns off from the balls/spools and take the skein off the niddy noddy. Next, cut through the skein where your strands ended. Now instead of a skein you should have a 5 or 6 foot long bunch of strands. Using good sharp scissors, start at one end of this bunch at cut through the bunch every 3 inches or so. (Longer if you want a shaggier yarn, shorter if you want a skinnier one.) Be sure that these cut sections lay on a flat surface and stay in a nice orderly row. You will not be able to spin them effectively if they are in a pile.
Note: Really short sections are harder to manage (1 to 1.5 inches), although they do look good once it's spun and they also fit through wheels with standard orifices. Just be forewarned!

-Choose two sturdy strings or threads for the "core".

Time to spin!
The basic concept behind this technique is that you will be sandwiching the cut sections of yarn between two core threads. As the threads spin together, the strands will be caught in between them and secured in the twist. continued......

41

Begin the yarn by spinning a lead section with any old roving and your two threads of choice.

Tip: Go for very sturdy material for the core threads, like bulky embroidery thread, thin yarn or string. A good source for this stuff is the thrift store, there are almost always old cones of thread and it's cheap too! Color doesn't matter as these threads won't show through the shag.

After a foot or so, leave off the roving and prepare to add some shag. Pinch the yarn where the roving ended and with your other hand separate the two threads. Carefully lay a small bunch of cut strands in between the two threads PERPENDICULAR to them. Like laying railroad tracks. Start the wheel spinning and with your thumb and forefinger guide the twist and make sure the strands stay centered on the thread. Once you have twisted through the row, tightly pinch the threads at the end of the stack to prevent untwisting. Separate the threads again, lay your next bunch of strands in and repeat this process. You will have to pull the shag yarn by hand through the orifice and wind it onto the bobbin, avoiding the guides. When your bobbin is full, pinch the end of the shag, add some roving and spin the core threads into a regular single yarn. You can use this section to tie the end of the shag yarn to the front for a complete skein.

Tip: Be careful how many strands you are spinning at one time. Too big a bunch will not twist tightly while too few will result in a scraggly looking shag.

SINGLES COIL

If you don't have a lot of patience and want a coily yarn but don't want to have to ply to get it, simply over spin your single!

Start spinning a single. After about six inches, keep spinning but hold the yarn so it does not get pulled onto the bobbin. You will see it start to coil up on itself. Help it along by using both hands to scrunch it together, constantly keeping it pinched at the end of the 6 inches. Once it is good and coiled let it wind onto the bobbin. Spin the next six inches the same way. Repeat.

Coiling is most effective when spun and bunched close to the orifice. The farther from the orifice you spin, the less coils you get.

You can do an entire yarn this way or just add it to a straight yarn to create textured sections.

BEEHIVE

Beehive in Contrasting Colors

Pre-Spinning Prep:

Start by choosing two wool rovings in contrasting colors. One color will make up the bulk of your yarn while the other will be sporadic spots (beehives) throughout.   Prepare the roving for spinning by stripping it apart into manageable pieces. The base color should be in easy to spin strips and the contrasting roving should be in pre-drafted sections approximately 1 inch by 4 inches. (The small sections should end up spinning the same diameter as the base yarn.)

A little extra preparation like this will make spinning go much faster!

Time to spin!

Start spinning your base color roving into a single. Every now and then spin in the small sections of contrasting roving. It is up to you how many of these little sections to add.   A few will result in a fairly even material with little beehives popping up here and there, while adding many will result in a very lumpy, bubbly material where the beehive color will tend to dominate.

Once your bobbin is full, replace it with a new one and prepare to ply in opposite direction from your single. Choose a sturdy sewing thread for plying. I like to use silk thread since it is stronger than cotton and has a nice shine to it.

The plying stage is the most important stage for creating the effect you want in this yarn. Take a little time to imagine what you want this yarn to look like. For the most dramatic effect the base yarn should be plied in a nice gentle wave to contrast with the tightly coiled Beehives. To do this you need to increase the tension so that the bobbin is taking the yarn in fairly fast and not putting a lot of twist in.   (But not so much tension that there is no twisting).   Use the first few yards that you spin to make these adjustments until you find a tension that is

comfortable and that gives the effect of a wiggly wave rather than a dense twist.   It is helpful to hold the thread tighter than the single, allowing the single to gently wrap around the thread.

Now for the beehive!
Ply the yarn in this manner until you get to the first small section of contrasting color. At this point switch the tension to the single rather than the thread. You will need to anchor the beehive by spinning the thread tightly for several turns at the point where the two colors meet.   You do this by bringing the single directly in front of the orifice (90degree) and spinning the thread in AT ONE POINT at a 90 degree angle to the yarn. 2 to 3 turns is plenty to keep the beehive from sliding up.

Return the thread to the straight position and ply the length of the contrasting color, stop at the bottom. Pinch the yarn where the two colors meet and push the single up the thread, making coils as it goes up. Keep the yarn pinched so that the twist does not continue down the yarn. Spin another anchor by putting the tension back on the single and feeding the thread in from the side again. Switch the thread back to the main position and continue the gentle plying until you reach the next contrasting section.

SUPER-COIL

See Beehive page 49

Once you know how to make the simple beehive, the Super-Coil is easy. It is basically one non-stop beehive.

Start with a single in any color/colors.

Choose a very strong thread, smooth string or yarn for plying (keep it skinny!).

Ply in the opposite direction from the single, keeping the tension on the thread. Do not allow the yarn to wind onto the bobbin. Ply the single for 3inches, then push it up the thread (just like making the beehive). Ply the next 3 inches, then push it up the thread so the coils sit right next to the last bunch. Repeat this action for a foot or so then let the coiled yarn wind onto the bobbin. (If the orifice or your guides are small you may have to hand wind a little.) Continue alternating bunching and winding for the entire yarn.

Tip: For a tightly coiled and even yarn ply for only 2 to 3 inches before bunching the coils. For a thick and thin coiled yarn, ply for 6 inches or so before bunching.

FLOWERS

Materials:
-uncarded wool locks in different colors, 3 to 5 inches (for the flowers).
-cream colored wool roving (for the base yarn)
-strong sewing thread (same colors as flowers).

Make the Flowers
You will want to make your flowers ahead of time so they are all ready to go when you sit down to spin. You can use uncarded locks from 3 to 5 inches depending on how big you want the flowers to be.
1) Separate the locks into sections for each flower, big sections for the "petals" and smaller,skinny sections for the centers.
2) Fold a skinny lock into a loop to form the center of the flower and wrap the larger wool lock around it for the petals. Pinching it together with one hand, pull some fibers out of BOTH locks to form a "stem".
3) Still pinching the flower together, take some thread and wrap it around the stem (just under the petals) tightly 3 or 4 times. Now, pinching the thread and stem together so the thread does not slacken, wrap the thread over the TOP of the flower 2 or 3 times tightly, separating the flower in half.
4) Wrap the thread around the stem again, once or twice, then over the top of the flower again PERPENDICU-LAR to your first wrap, dividing the flower into quarters. This will give you your four petals.
5) Finish the flower by giving a couple more wraps around the stem and tying the two ends of thread off in a knot. Leave a few inches of thread at each end to spin into the base yarn. Split the "stem" fibers and thread into two. Draft these fibers out well, so that they readily spin into the base yarn. These two sections are very important, one will be spun to the base yarn ahead of the flower, and one behind- securely attaching the flower to the yarn.

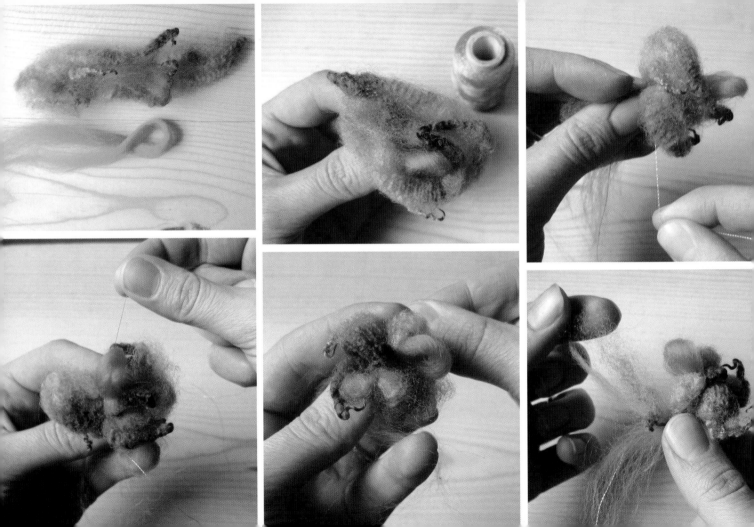

Time to spin!
Now that the flowers are done, this is the easy part!

Spin your roving as usual , when you are ready to add a flower simply spin in, leading with one of the split "stem" sections, making sure to keep the roving pinched at the flower (so the twist does not get ahead of you!). Spin tightly up to the flower, then slowly moving your hand back behind the flower, let the second part of the split stem spin into the base roving. Make sure you get plenty of twist around these guys! Now you just keep spinning, adding as many or as few flowers as you want.

Tip: You can spin this yarn on a standard wheel, but you need to use your threading hook to pull the flowers through the orifice. After the flower is securely spun onto the yarn, take the hook and insert it into the orifice *from the bobbin side*. When it pops out your side of the orifice hook it around the center of the flower. Use the hook to pull the flower gently though the orifice. It helps to also pull the base yarn from the bobbin side as well. Do not drag the flower through the guides, hand wind them on to the bobbin. It is ok for the yarn to get wound on top of the flowers on the bobbin, they will pop out later.

Do not forget to set the twist or these flowers will fall right out!

COTTON BALLS

Materials:
-Silk Hanks (These look just like a package of silk hankies!)
-Wool roving

You will need to spin this yarn on a Quill as the silk balls are very delicate. Many companies offer a separate Quill attachment for your wheel. If you use a standard wheel carefully pull the balls through the orifice with the threading hook and gently wind them onto the bobbin by hand. You can re-shape the balls after soaking and setting the twist.

Make the "Cotton Balls":
Using some dense carded roving, roll a chunk of wool between your palms to form a semi-felted sphere about the size of a cotton ball. (Just as you would with clay or cookie dough.) Roll at least 10.
Gently remove a layer of silk from the stack of hanks. Make sure you only have one layer, they are very hard to separate and are incredibly thin. The easiest way is to start at a corner and gently pry a layer up. Once you have a single hank, lay it on your open hand, place one wool ball on top and grab the ball in your hand, covering it with the silk. Pinch the silk together and make one twist sealing the wool inside. Pinching the silk tightly at the base of the ball, tear the rest of the silk hank away, leaving only the covered ball and a long tail of torn silk fibers. Use some muscle! Silk is a very strong fiber and does not tear easily. Repeat until all balls are covered.

Time to spin!
Spin a simple single with the wool and periodically spin a "Cotton Ball" in by splitting the wool, inserting the ragged end of the silk ball into the split and spinning tightly up to and beyond the ball.

UNCARDED

Spinning uncarded wool may be simple and easy but the end result can be very dramatic.

To prepare uncarded wool simply fluff up the locks slightly by hand before spinning, then spin as you would combed or carded roving. For extra texture allow the tips of the locks to remain unspun, sticking out of the yarn sporadically.

For extra shaggy yarn, spin only the base of the lock into the yarn leaving an inch or two to stand out. Be careful not to separate the end fibers so the original shape of the lock remains.

TREASURE BOX

A treasure box yarn takes several months to make as it consists of many individual, special and beautiful little elements collected and carefully saved. As you are going through your fiber, always keep your eyes open for particularly nice little bits that seem to somehow magically appear in your stash. These precious gems might be semi-felted bits from an old roll of wool, or perhaps a little sparkle fiber got balled up with a strand of novelty yarn. When you find these nuggets, set them aside in a safe place. Over time the Treasure Box will become full and then you will have enough material to make a surprising and beautiful yarn.

Empty the treasure box out and look over what you have. Choose a roving for the bulk of the yarn that compliments your collection. Then simply begin spinning, adding in the little gems one at a time throughout the yarn.

Tip: Don't limit yourself to the fiber box when looking for treasure. The world is full of tiny lovely things. You can find bits for your treasure box on the street, in the thrift store, in nature, anywhere.

*See page 62 to see what these yarns look like crocheted!

BEYOND SPINNING...
Treasure Hat
Ana Voog - On Freeform Crochet

Freeform is about creating things as you go along and not following pre-made patterns. One of the most common questions I hear from those who wish to learn to freeform is: "How can I create exactly what I envision in my head?". The answer to that question is that it isn't very often that an artist can make exactly what they see in their head. The sooner you can let go of your expectations for something to be what you want it to be, the more the act of creation will flow and take you on a journey of exploration. Instead of asking "How can I make this be what I see in my head", ask "What will happen if I let this be what it wants to be?". Strangely, one of the best ways to do this is to leave all of your mistakes and incorporate them into your work. I like to call mistakes "beautiful accidents" or serendipity.

You do not need to have any special skill to freeform. 99% of all my hats are created by using only the single stitch. Any shape you can imagine can be created and the more you practice the more you will get the hang of it. Don't be discouraged if what you make doesn't meet your expectations. Say what you make looks like a sad pancake, that's good! Go with it. Make a sad pancake hat. Even make lots of sad pancakes and then hook them all up together and see what that looks like and where that will take you. Allow your "mistakes" to take you on adventures. Instead of saying "What IS that? It's not what I expected.", say "What could this BE? what would happen if...".

For me, freeform is about loving the process, the journey. It's not about getting anywhere in particular, but immersing yourself in the process of "now", which is from where the well of creativity springs. It's about letting go of all expectations and just being. Don't worry about making things the "right" way, make things YOUR way! You have nothing to lose and everything to gain. At the very worst, you will make a sad pancake hat with soul. Have HUMOUR in all you do, that is also essential. Laugh at your sad pancake hat like you laugh at your dog who sleeps upside down. After all is said and done, it is things like these which are the most precious bits to life.

63

SPECIAL THANKS

Thanks to Ana Voog for creating the wonderful Treasure Hat and for constantly and beautifully blurring the line between art and craft. To Laura Hartwick, Design Trainer Extraordinaire, for helping to get my scattered information into a bonafide book. To Elle and Kathy, my oldest customers and great craftsmen, two people who's very lives are an inspiration. To Jenny Neutron Star, my spinning compatriot on the frontline of the Handspun Revolution. To Lou, for teaching me how to spin and keeping the world's best little yarn shop. And finally- Thanks to every single one of you fabulous yarn lovers who I have come to know through Pluckyfluff.com. This book is for you guys and I hope to see all of your new creations soon.

CONTRIBUTORS

Ana Voog is an artist who works with many mediums: music, photography, painting, performance art, crochet, sewing and writing. Her creations can be viewed at: www.anacam.com
She can be contacted at ana@voog.com

*Photo of "Treaure Box Hat" taken by Ana Voog.